Deserts

ENDANGERED PEOPLE & PLACES

Deserts

BY MARTIN JENKINS

Photographs by Still Pictures

Lerner Publications Company • Minneapolis

All words that appear in **bold** are explained in the glossary on page 46.

Map by European Map Graphics Ltd. Photographs on pp. 14-15 by Royal Geographical Society; pp. 36-37 by Science Photo Library; pp. 20, 21, 24-25, 38 by ZEFA Picture Library; all other photographs by Still Pictures.

This edition first published in the United States in 1996 by Lerner Publications Company, 241 First Avenue North, Minneapolis, MN 55401.
Copyright © 1995 Cherrytree Press Ltd.

Library of Congress Cataloging-in-Publication Data
Jenkins, Martin.
    Deserts / by Martin Jenkins.
    p.   cm. — (Endangered people and places)
    Includes index.
    Summary: Discusses desert people, climate, landscape, plants, animals, and present and future threats to them.
    ISBN 0-8225-2775-8 (lib. bdg. : alk. paper)
    1. Deserts—Juvenile literature. 2. Nomads—Juvenile literature. 3. Desert ecology—Juvenile literature. [1. Deserts. 2. Nomads. 3. Desert ecology. 4. Ecology.] I. Title. II. Series.
GF55.J45 1996
333.73'6—dc20   95–25401
                                                         CIP
                                                          AC

Printed in Italy by L.E.G.O. s.p.a., Vicenza
Bound in the United States of America
1 2 3 4 5 6 01 00 99 98 97 96

CONTENTS

THE DESERT WORLD

Deserts are not the lifeless expanses of land that many people imagine. Plants, animals, and humans have all adapted to living in deserts since prehistoric times. In fact, some of the oldest known human remains come from desert areas.

Deserts cover more than one-third of the earth's land surface. About one out of every ten people in the the world lives in deserts. In some places, people follow nearly the same lifestyle as early desert dwellers did. A large number of people, for instance, are still **nomads,** moving from place to place with their animals, homes, and other belongings.

Life in the desert is harsh. Food and water are hard to find. But desert dwellers have developed useful ways of making the best of the scarce resources. As a result, these people are able to survive from the natural bounty of the desert.

Deserts in the Modern World

The influence of the modern world has extended to some deserts. New uses have been found for the arid (dry) lands, including mining, tourism, ranching, and farming. These changes have affected the lives of traditional desert peoples.

Deserts are harsh but fragile places. To sustain desert environments, humans need to recognize the impact of their actions, small and large. Desert peoples, who have successfully survived desert life by following age-old practices, can guide us in this quest.

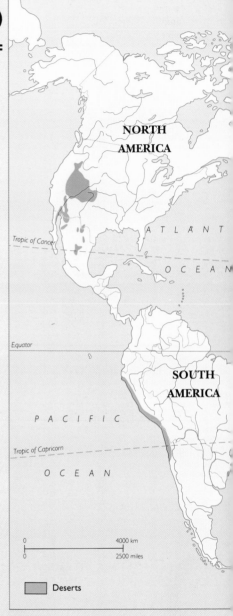

Right: Sand dunes blanket the Sahara, a region of deserts in North Africa. Sand dunes cover about one-fifth of the total area of the world's deserts. Dunes range in size from small ridges less than 3 feet (1 meter) high to enormous hills of sand over 1,200 feet (350 m) tall and a half a mile (800 m) across. In some places, large dunes gather to form enormous seas of sand called *ergs.* Very little lives in these ergs, which are some of the most barren places on earth.

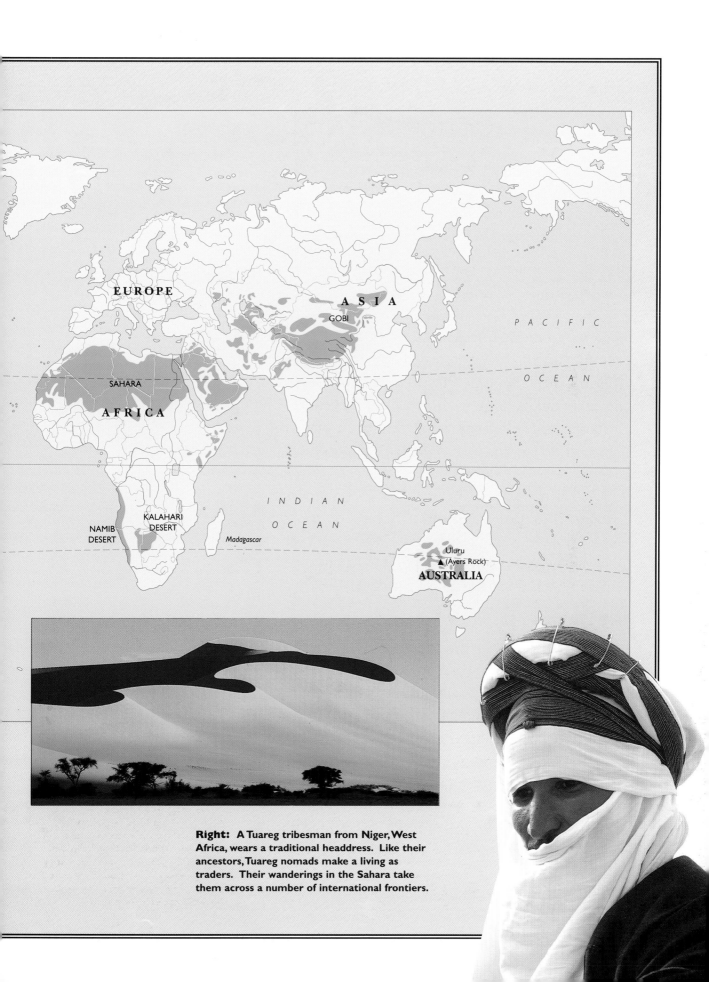

EUROPE

ASIA

GOBI

PACIFIC

OCEAN

SAHARA

AFRICA

INDIAN

OCEAN

NAMIB
DESERT

KALAHARI
DESERT

Madagascar

Uluru
▲ (Ayers Rock)

AUSTRALIA

Right: A Tuareg tribesman from Niger, West Africa, wears a traditional headdress. Like their ancestors, Tuareg nomads make a living as traders. Their wanderings in the Sahara take them across a number of international frontiers.

TYPES OF DESERT

All deserts have one thing in common—a shortage of water. Arid lands receive less than 10 inches (25 centimeters) of precipitation (rain, snow, and hail) a year. When rain does come, it is usually irregular. In some areas, no rain falls for years. Then, several inches may suddenly pound the dry land in less than 24 hours. Desert animals, plants, and people have had to adapt to an unpredictable supply of water.

Desert Variety

Although they are all dry, deserts can differ in other ways. Deserts may be largely sandy, stony, or covered in pebbles. Arid lands may be flat and featureless or rolling and hilly. They may be full of cliffs, canyons, and unique rock formations. Some deserts, such as Death Valley in California, lie below sea level. Others, including the Chihuahua Desert in Mexico, rest high up on plateaus and in mountains. Most of the Tibetan Plateau desert, in central Asia, is more than 15,000 feet (4,500 m) above sea level.

Many deserts sit in the middle of continents, far from a coast. However, deserts such as the Atacama in northern Chile and southern Peru and the Namib Desert in southern Africa border a sea. Despite being right next to an ocean, these seashore deserts are among the driest places on earth.

Desert Climate

Because desert landscapes and locations vary, deserts can have different climates. Although we

SHAPING THE LAND

The surface of a desert is constantly being eroded (worn away) by the

The Sahara, the largest desert in the world, is probably also the hottest. The highest surface temperature ever recorded (136° F/ 58° C) was in the Sahara, in Libya.

usually think of deserts as hot places, they can also be cold, especially at night. Mountain deserts, such as the Tibetan Plateau, remain freezing all day long in the wintertime and often stay cool during the day, even at the height of summer.

The Namib Fog Desert
The Namib Desert runs for more than 750 miles (1,200 kilometers) along the Atlantic coast of Namibia in southern Africa. The northern section of the desert, called the Skeleton Coast, receives no rain for years. Instead, for 60 to 80 days of the year, a wet fog rolls in from the Atlantic Ocean during the early morning. This fog leaves behind a heavy dew, from which the desert's plants and animals obtain the water they need.

The Spiny Desert of Madagascar
Madagascar is a large island in the Indian Ocean off the southeastern coast of Africa. The island, isolated from the rest of the world for tens of millions of years, contains many animals and plants found nowhere else. In the desert area of southwestern Madagascar, which sometimes receives less than two inches (five centimeters) of rain a year, unique cacti grow. These spiny plants are quickly being destroyed, however, as workers cut them down to make charcoal or to clear the land for cattle grazing.

action of wind and water. Water, when it comes, can carve through hard rock. The Grand Canyon in Arizona was formed over a period of millions of years, as the Colorado River eroded the desert surface. **Erosion** by water is a powerful force in deserts, where little vegetation exists to keep soil in place.

Much of the sand in deserts comes from grains of eroded rock called sediments. When picked up by the wind, sediments become strong erosion agents themselves. Small particles carried by the wind grind away at rock surfaces, sculpting them into unique shapes, such as this rock formation in the Sahara in Algeria.

9

DESERT PLANTS

Like most creatures that have adapted to the extreme weather conditions of deserts, plants have ways of coping with the shortage of water. Perhaps the most familiar desert plants are **succulents,** which store water to carry them through **droughts,** or long periods with no rain.

The best-known succulents are from the cactus family. Cacti usually have thickened stems and no leaves and are covered with a mass of thorns and prickles. The stems store water and the prickles protect the plants from being eaten by large animals. Many cacti have roots that do not grow deep in the ground but are spread over a wide area. When it does rain, the roots can absorb as much water as possible.

Some succulents with thickened stems look like cacti but belong to other plant families. Many succulents have thickened leaves or large, swollen **tubers** (underground stems). Desert trees have roots that go far down to tap **groundwater,** or water that has seeped and collected deep underground. Because these plants do not have to store water, they do not usually have swollen leaves or stems.

The Desert in Bloom

A number of plants, called **ephemerals,** have found a different way of avoiding drought. They spend most of their lives as seeds lying on or just below the desert surface. The seeds have hard outer casings that resist heat. During a drought, ephemerals remain alive as seeds but do not actively grow. They can stay in this dormant state for years. After a heavy rainfall, however, they sprout, grow, flower, produce more seeds, and die— all in the short time it takes for the ground to dry out again. Usually many different species of desert plants do this at once, transforming the desert into a multi-colored carpet of flowers spreading for miles in all directions.

Above: Flowering plants cover a desert in Arizona. Rain rarely comes to desert areas, but when it does the desert blooms. Many desert plants have only a few weeks in which to grow, flower, and seed. The plants might have to wait years before the next rain.

Right: A welwitschia, a primitive plant related to pine trees, grows in the Namib Desert. The welwitschia looks like no other plant. It produces only two leaves that may split lengthwise as they grow. Some large welwitschia are hundreds of years old. Like many other plants in the Namib Desert, the welwitschia gets its water from the sea fogs.

THE CACTUS RUSTLERS

Because they are unique, cacti and other succulents are sought after by people wanting to decorate their gardens and buildings. But many of these plants are so rare and fragile that they are protected by law. Nevertheless, in the United States and in other parts of the world some people make their living by cactus rustling—illegally digging up cacti at night and smuggling them out of the desert in trucks.

Some of the most coveted cacti are several hundred years old when they are dug up. People have been known to pay up to $5,000 for a Saguaro cactus measuring 10 feet (3 m) in height. Not long after being removed from their environment, however, cacti often die, and the rustlers are kept busy finding replacements. But as rustling continues, many plants, especially the older cacti, become harder to replace.

Other people collect rare cacti and other succulents. Although nowadays most of these plants can be raised from seed or cuttings in nurseries, some collectors prefer to own plants taken from the wild. Succulents from Mexico, Africa, and the southwestern United States are particularly popular. Some species are only found in one or two places, making them even more desirable to collectors and more prone to extinction. Many of the rare cacti are small and slow growing. A plant the size of a tea plate may be more than 100 years old.

Most of these rare plants are protected by law in the countries where they grow, but it is difficult to stop people from collecting them. The small ones are easy to smuggle out in suitcases, or even in the mail, to countries such as Britain, Germany, and Japan. At least one type of Mexican cactus is thought to have become extinct in the wild because of this illegal activity.

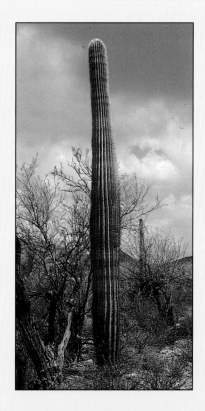

Above: Cacti are found in deserts of the southwestern United States. Apart from one species that lives in Africa, cacti all originate from North and South America and from the Caribbean. However some cacti, particularly prickly pears, now grow wild in other parts of the world and have become a menace in countries such as Australia and Madagascar.

Right: Wild millet is sometimes found in the Sahara. Many farmers in Africa raise millet, which thrives in dry areas, as a cereal crop. But the grain is not often found growing wild.

11

DESERT ANIMALS

Like plants, desert animals have evolved to be able to handle a desert's heat and lack of water. Small animals stay underground in burrows during the day, coming out only at night when it is cool. Larger animals such as antelopes seek shade for shelter during the hottest part of the day. Some animals dig a hollow depression in the ground and lie in the cooler, unexposed soil.

Below: A fennec fox peeps from its burrow in the Sahara. Like many desert animals, fennec foxes are nocturnal, coming out from their cool burrows only at night to hunt. The foxes have sharp hearing and use it to track down beetles, grasshoppers, lizards, and small mammals for food. The fennec fox also loses body heat through its large ears, helping it stay cool.

Above: The fearsome-looking moloch, or thorny devil, is a lizard only about 6 inches (15 cm) long. It lives in deserts in Australia and feeds on ants. The lizard's armored spikes deter predators. Its brown and yellow coloring camouflage it in the sands and pebbles of the desert surface. The moloch's body temperature, like that of other reptiles, depends on the temperature of the air. During the night when the air is cool, the lizard's body temperature drops and it becomes very sluggish. At dawn the lizard moves out into the sun, warms up, and becomes active. It usually finds shelter in the shade at midday, however, when the desert sun is too hot even for the moloch.

Dealing with Drought

Most desert animals can survive on small amounts of water. Many animals do not drink but get all the water they need from their food. Others drink occasionally, perhaps once a week. These are usually larger mammals, such as gazelles and wild goats, as well as birds. These creatures often have to travel considerable distances to find water at isolated springs and waterholes.

Ground Heat

Animals that do venture out during the day have to be able to tolerate the intense heat of the ground, which can be far hotter than the air. The sand cat, which lives in deserts in North Africa and the Middle East, has hairy pads on its paws to protect them from the hot ground. The pads also give the cat a solid grip when walking on sand dunes. The sidewinder rattlesnake from North America loops sideways across the sand, only keeping a small part of its belly in contact with the ground at any one time. Some South African lizards stand on only three, or even two, legs at a time, holding the others above ground until the feet in use become too hot. The constant swapping of legs makes the lizards appear to be performing exercises or a strange, slow dance.

Left: A scarab beetle. Many types of beetles and other insects live in deserts. Their hard outer skin helps them to conserve water. Because these beetles are small, they easily find shelter from the heat of the sun. Scarab beetles usually feed on vegetation and dung, although some will also eat carrion—the remains of dead animals. Beetles are an important part of the diet of many larger desert animals, including fennec foxes.

THE LIVES OF DESERT PEOPLES

From the most hostile conditions, desert dwellers have fashioned a life that is plentiful, both materially and culturally. Generation after generation, they have handed down their knowledge about desert survival. The way of life for some desert peoples has continued almost unchanged for hundreds and sometimes thousands of years.

As a result, desert peoples from around the world have made long-lasting contributions to culture. Some of the world's religions took root in these arid lands. For the spiritually minded, the desert has been a place of purity. Some people test the strength of their religious beliefs by spending time suffering in the heat of a desert.

In ancient days, deserts formed almost impassable barriers between different civilizations. What little contact there was resulted from the help and guidance given to travelers by desert dwellers. All contact between China and Europe before the fifteenth century, for example, was through desert caravans. These groups of traders and pack animals traveled in large numbers for safety. Many caravans crossed the Gobi Desert along the famous **Silk Road.**

Below: Tuareg tribesmen ride their camels in the Sahara near Djanet, Algeria. A similar scene could have been witnessed hundreds of years ago.

LIVING IN THE DESERT

In desert regions, plants, animals, and water can be found but are scattered over huge areas. People who live in deserts have had to adopt to a similar strategy if they are to survive. Traditional desert life, in many parts of the world, is nomadic. To make the best of the scarce resources, desert peoples travel over a defined territory, taking care never to exhaust or destroy a particular resource.

Some desert dwellers live by hunting and gathering. Small groups of people range over large distances, living off the varied wild resources of the desert. The Australian Aborigines and the San (called Bushmen by Europeans) of the Kalahari Desert in southern Africa are typical hunter-gatherers.

Pastoral nomadism is more complex. This way of life involves keeping large herds of animals, usually camels, sheep, or goats, and grazing them on desert vegetation. Along the edges of some deserts, where vegetation increases, herders keep cattle, too.

Portable Homes

Because they have beasts of burden, pastoral nomads can carry much more than hunter-gatherers. Pastoral nomads carry everything they need, including their homes. A nomad's home is uaually a lightweight tent made out of tightly woven wool or animal skins. The dwelling is supported on a wooden frame and held in place by ropes. As they wander over large distances, pastoral nomads maintain contacts with settled communities. The nomads trade milk and cheese for goods that they cannot make themselves, such as pots and pans.

Permanent Settlements

Not all desert peoples are nomadic. In places where water is available year-round, desert dwellers have built settlements with more permanent homes. The earliest permanent homes in deserts were caves. Caves were used by people in the northern part of the Sahara and by the Anasazi Indians in what is now the southwestern United States. The Anasazi built their cave towns more than 1,000 years ago. Their descendants are the Pueblo Indians, who until very recently still lived in much the

DESERT HOMES

Because few trees grow in deserts, wood is in short supply. Instead of lumber, people use stone or baked mud or clay to build permanent dwellings.

In North Africa and in the Arabian Peninsula, whole cities have been made out of mud-brick buildings several stories high. These structures would not survive for long in a wet climate, where rain would gradually dissolve them. But in dry areas, mud-brick buildings can remain standing for centuries and can easily be repaired if they are damaged.

Desert homes usually have thick walls and small windows and doors to shield the interiors from the heat of the day and the chill of the night. In a similar way, people who live in deserts wear special clothing to protect themselves from the elements.

Right: Nomads in western Mongolia live in tents called *gers,* which are made of hides and canvas wrapped around circular wooden frames. Easy to transport and assemble, gers are also windproof.

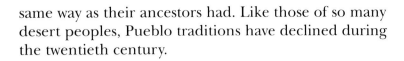
Left: A mosque built from mud stands sturdy in Mali, a country in the western Sahara. Mud buildings can endure for centuries in desert climates.

Below: Tents made from animal skins are common in Timbuktu, Mali.

same way as their ancestors had. Like those of so many desert peoples, Pueblo traditions have declined during the twentieth century.

Desert Clothing

Daytime temperatures in the Sahara and on the Arabian Peninsula can be well over 100° F (40° C). People in these areas wear long loose robes that cover their bodies. This type of clothing protects desert dwellers from the blazing sun and allows air to circulate underneath, helping them to keep cool.

Farther south, where temperatures are not as extreme, desert dwellers wear fewer clothes. The San of the Kalahari and the Australian Aborigines wear very little. Their bodies are well adapted to heat and sunshine, although they usually avoid the hottest parts of the day. These desert peoples sometimes tolerate the cold at night by wrapping themselves in animal skins. In colder areas, such as the Gobi in Mongolia, people wear many layers of tightly woven woolen cloth and thick animal furs to keep warm in the bitter winds that howl across the plains.

PEOPLE OF THE KALAHARI

Of all deserts, the Kalahari probably offers the least hostile conditions for humans. Water is never far below the surface. Although clearly a desert, the Kalahari supports plenty of **savanna** vegetation, including trees, bushes, and grasses. A few patches of the desert are even forested.

The Kalahari is famous for the San, a people whose way of life had, until recently, changed little since the Stone Age. The San are short in stature. The men are about 5 feet (150 cm) tall on average, and the women are slightly shorter. The San speak a number of languages that contain clicking sounds difficult for non-San to imitate.

Hunter-Gatherers

The San once lived all over southern Africa, but their lands were gradually reduced by Bantu-speaking herders. During the 1800s, the San were hunted down by Dutch settlers who wanted their lands. The San took refuge in the Kalahari.

In the Kalahari, the San gained an extraordinary knowledge of the land and became experts at tracking game and finding water. The San sometimes stored water beneath the sand in empty ostrich-egg shells. Food

Above: A prehistoric rock engraving of a giraffe made by San in Namibia, Africa.

Right: These San have been forced off their traditional land. They now do farm work for low wages in order to have enough to eat.

Left: An elderly San sucks nourishment from a root. The San who still follow a traditional way of life depend on a huge variety of desert plants and animals for a healthy diet.

came from hunting wild animals and from gathering berries, nuts, and tubers. The San traveled widely, ranging over areas of up to 400 square miles (1,000 sq km), in groups of about 25 people.

Traveling Light

With so far to travel and no pack animals, the San hauled few possessions. What they did have included weapons such as wooden spears and bows and arrows. The people also carried water bags and wooden bowls for gathering berries.

When the San needed shelter, they made dwellings out of tree branches covered with bark, twigs, or grass. Sometimes they spent the night in a cave or under a rock overhang. During the Kalahari winter, the San often made more permanent wood and grass homes, in which they remained for several weeks.

Hunting

The men usually did the hunting, tracking down animals and approaching as near as possible before shooting them with poison-tipped arrows. The women collected berries, which formed an important part of the San diet. Studies of the San have shown that their diet was extremely good and their food obtained with little effort. Their plentiful spare time was filled up with chatting, singing and dancing, or listening to traditional myths as recounted by master storytellers around campfires.

Twentieth-Century Problems

Of the 55,000 or so San who now live in the Kalahari, few still survive by hunting and gathering. Even nowadays, people want San land for mining and cattle ranching. Only about 2,000 San still live in the region in the same way that their ancestors did. Many San have now settled in townships. But hunter-gatherers find the modern world bewildering. Divorced from their lands and their traditional activities, some San have developed serious social problems, such as alcoholism.

Above: Roots and tubers are a source of water and nourishment for the San. The task of gathering plants was generally done by the women of the group, while the men hunted animals.

ABORIGINES OF AUSTRALIA

In many ways, the life of the Australian Aborigines was similar to that of the San. Until British colonists arrived in Australia in the eighteenth century, Aboriginal people lived throughout the continent, mostly in the coastal regions where the climate was more moderate than in the great arid interior. Nevertheless, a number of tribes eked out a living in these desert areas.

True Nomads

The Aborigines of the desert were truly nomadic, wandering over large areas in small groups. Like the San, the Aborigines survived by hunting wild animals and collecting fruit, tubers, and other edible plant matter. Again like the San, the men did the hunting and the women gathered the plant foods.

On their travels, the Aborigines carried very little—usually just weapons such as spears and boomerangs and a few tools made of wood, stone, or bone. The most important of these was a hard, sharp-pointed digging stick, which the women used for digging up tubers and sometimes as a weapon to defend themselves. The Aborigines left bigger implements, such as grinding stones, at major campsites.

Above: Rock paintings and engravings by Australian Aboriginal peoples date back te of thousands of years. Most of them ages depict people, as well as the animals they hunted. Other drawings contain mysterious figures that probably represent magical spirits.

Right: Apart from its uses for cooking and providing warmth, fire is an important resource for Aborigines. Here, a hunter uses a fire to harden the points of his wooden spears. The Aborigines sometimes start bush fires to flush out game and to encourage new growth.

Above: A group of Aborigines at a *corroboree*, a gathering that involves storytelling, music, and dancing. Corroborees were important for maintaining friendships and allegiances between the smaller groups of Aborigines.

Protection from the Heat

Because of the hot climate in the desert, the Aborigines wore little or no clothing. Their dark skins protected them from sunburn and their bodies tolerated both the heat of the desert day and the cool of the night. Nevertheless, the Aborigines sought the shade of a tree or an overhanging rock during the hottest part of the day. They made campfires and blankets of tree bark to keep warm on cold nights.

Aborigine Art

The Aborigines developed sophisticated decorative art. Their elaborate abstract paintings, inspired by ancient cave paintings, are a means of connecting with "dreamtime," which for the Aborigines is the period when all life began. These paintings are now collected worldwide. Some modern Aboriginal paintings sell for large sums of money.

Aborigines Today

For Aborigines contact with white settlers has for the most part been disastrous. In the past, newcomers shot many Aborigines. Otherwise, they were encouraged to abandon their nomadic life for a more European lifestyle. Divorced from their past but with no role in the newcomers' world, the Aborigines became social misfits.

After decades of suffering, Aborigines have begun to redress a few of the injustices done to them. The Aborigines have gotten the Australian government, for example, to accept Aboriginal claims to land of spiritual and cultural significance. The Aborigines can once again retreat to Uluru (formerly Ayers Rock), the largest single piece of stone in the world and a place of spiritual importance to the Aborigines.

The government has also given Aborigines more control in deciding their own affairs. The Aboriginal Development Commission now has an all Aboriginal board of directors and receives millions of dollars every year for housing, low-cost loans, and enterprise schemes. Some 2,000 Aboriginal organizations get some form of government support.

Tuareg People of the Sahara

Below: A veiled Tuareg youth rides a camel in the Sahara.

The largest desert in the world, the Sahara stretches for 4,375 miles (7,040 km) from east to west and 1,562 miles (2,513 km) from north to south. Its land is shared by 11 nation-states and many peoples, including Berbers, Dogon, and Wodaabe. Foremost among such peoples are the Tuareg, a nomadic tribe numbering about one million individuals.

The Tuareg, whose male members often wear a distinctive blue veil, refer to themselves as Kel Taligmust, or the People of the Veil. The Tuareg are the most ancient inhabitants of the Sahara. For centuries, they have practiced a nomadic or seminomadic way of life, raising and living off camels, goats, sheep, and cattle in the central Saharan region. Through their intimate knowledge of navigating the desert, the Tuareg controlled the cross-Saharan trade—a position they sometimes abused. Riding their swift camels, the Tuareg raided trade caravans. Beginning in the 1890s, the Tuareg began to extract salt from the desert, using it to trade for grain.

Although the Tuareg are divided into several groups and scattered over a wide area, they all speak the same language and share a common cultural heritage. Initially reluctant to adopt Islam when the religion spread to the region in the seventh and eighth centuries, the Tuareg are now devout Muslims.

Tuareg Society

Tuareg society is divided into nobles, vassals, and slaves. For centuries, nobles controlled the caravan routes, the vassals were the herders, and the slaves grew crops and did menial work such as saddling the camels. In spite of this, the Tuareg are not a submissive people. They are proud, independent, and in some ways egalitarian. It is said that no Tuareg kneels when his chief passes, and, indeed, the chief is removable at any time.

Modern life has brought difficulties for the Tuareg. Their traditional activities have come under

Above: A Tuareg family gathers outside their dwelling.

Below: Traditional and modern combine at a Tuareg wedding ceremony. Guests carry wedding presents of radio and cassette players.

Above: A Tuareg woman fills camel-hide waterskins at a well.

increasing strain. Air transport has replaced the caravan. Their salt is no longer wanted and their grazing lands have been gradually taken away. Tuareg territory cuts across the boundaries of six independent nation-states: Mali, Burkina Faso, Mauritania, Niger, Algeria, and Libya. Their independent spirit has brought them into conflict with these states. A low-intensity guerrilla warfare may continue until the Tuareg feel they have their freedom.

Desert People of North America

The European settlement of North and South America marked the beginning of a tragic age for the indigenous peoples. For most of the continents' original inhabitants, contact with settlers spelled the end of traditional ways of life.

Because they lived in a tough, arid terrain, the desert tribes of North America fared slightly better than other groups. The desert lands of the Hopi and the Navajo Indians of what is now the southwestern United States, for example, held fewer attractions for European colonists.

The Hopi lived in clifftop villages in houses built of stone and rendered with clay. For defense purposes, few of the houses had doors. Instead, ladders were used to climb onto the roofs, from which point the rooms could be entered. The Hopi farmed corn, a crop that formed a central part of their culture and religious life. "Corn is the heart of the Hopi," went a local proverb.

The Navajo

By contrast the Navajo were mainly a hunting and gathering people and lived in more scattered communities than the Hopi. Fierce fighters, the Navajo raided the more peaceable Hopi for food and goods. In

Above: Cliff Palace at Mesa Verde National Park in Colorado contains hundreds of rooms. These ancient cliff dwellings were designed between 1100 and 1300 by early desert peoples called the **Anasazi**.

winter the Navajo inhabited small, one-roomed houses called hogans. The homes, in which the Navajo performed healing ceremonies, were central to the group's religion. Navajo were skilled jewelers, working mainly with silver and turquoise. Nowadays, Navajo-style jewelry is a popular fashion accessory.

Nevertheless, contact with the Europeans eventually affected the desert dwellers of North America. Spaniards tried to impose the Catholic faith on the Hopi, who rebelled. Many Hopi fled to live with the Navajo and, over time, the two groups adopted one another's customs.

Numbering about 150,000, the Navajo are now the largest Native American group in the United States. Many of them live on **reservations** in Arizona, New Mexico, and Utah. Some tribal members herd sheep and goats, although the land is heavily overgrazed. Other Navajo make their living by weaving blankets and crafting jewelry. Widespread social problems, including chronic unemployment, are major complications of reservation life.

COLD DESERTS OF ASIA

Several desert regions stretch across Asia but the largest and best-known is the Gobi. The Gobi is made up of several distinct arid regions that span southeastern Mongolia and northern China. The fifth largest desert area in the world, the Gobi is also one of the most hostile, with temperatures as low as -40° F (-40° C) in winter and as high as 113° F (45° C) in summer. The word Gobi is derived from the Mongolian term for "waterless place."

The seminomadic Khalkha Mongols make up the largest tribal group in the Gobi. They herd sheep and goats, but their mainstay is the two-humped Bactrian camel. About 600,000 of these camels live in the Gobi. They provide desert dwellers with many necessities, including meat, milk, wool, hides for tents, and dung for fuel. In addition, the Bactrian camel is an extremely hardy beast of burden, capable of carrying 440 pounds (200 kilograms) for long distances under extreme conditions.

The nomads of the Gobi live in domed circular tents called gers, which are made of skins and cloth tied over a wooden frame. The many layers of material provide good insulation against freezing temperatures.

Above: Mongols in the southern Gobi serve tea to celebrate the mare's first milk of the year.

Below: A herdsboy in central Mongolia brings in calves for the night.

Above: A Mongol family poses in their ger, which is decorated with brightly colored rugs.

BACTRIAN CAMEL

The Bactrian camel—the so-called Ship of the Desert—is a hardy desert animal. It can go for days without water. It can survive on coarse desert vegetation and can walk for miles through the hot sun without becoming overheated. The camel's broad, flat feet stop it from sinking into the soft sand, while its long eyelashes and special nostril-flaps keep sand and grit out of its eyes and nose during sandstorms. The Bactrian camel supplies desert peoples with milk and meat, hair for weaving into cloth, skin for tents and bags, and transport for people and their belongings.

Uses and Abuses of Deserts

Deserts provide a living for large numbers of people as well as many benefits for those who reside far away. Deserts are also fragile places that can easily be abused. Traditional desert peoples learned over the years how much they could take out of the land without destroying it. But because more people are coming to deserts, this situation has changed dramatically.

Aircraft and four-wheel-drive vehicles have placed even the most remote areas of desert within the reach of humans. Indigenous desert dwellers now find themselves in the company of tourists, hunters, soldiers, traders, and mineral prospectors. In their different ways, all these newcomers affect the desert environment, either through sheer weight of numbers of because of the activities they are engaged in. Also, newcomers to desert areas often do not understand how deserts work.

The traditional inhabitants of deserts have changed, too. Their populations have increased greatly, placing more pressure on the land. The digging of new boreholes and wells encourages people to keep more livestock, which may overgraze the land around the wells and cause erosion. Such problems need to be overcome both to preserve desert environments and to prevent the desert from encroaching on less arid regions.

Below: Cattle drink from a waterhole in Niger. Although cattle are not well adapted to living in deserts, the animals traditionally are kept in large numbers in semidesert areas, such as here in the Sahel, a dry region south of the Sahara in North Africa. The tribes who herd cattle are nomadic. They move with their herds to find grazing areas.

Right: In the United States, desert areas such as Nevada are popular destinations for tourists. Good roads and mobile homes enable vacationers to easily cross deserts. Like traditional nomads, these modern-day nomads can carry their homes, food, and water with them. However, unlike true nomads, most of these travelers have permanent homes to return to.

MODERN LIFE IN DESERTS

As in other areas of the world, life in deserts has been greatly changed by modern technology. The Tuareg are just as comfortable behind the wheel of a pickup truck as they are riding a camel. Even isolated desert communities have contact with the outside world through radios, telephones, and television.

New Desert Dwellers

Modern towns in deserts are often built of imported materials, such as corrugated iron, rather than local clay or stone. The inhabitants of these towns are often not traditional desert dwellers. In many parts of the world, the dry climate and endless sunshine have attracted new groups to deserts, including vacationers, retirees, and companies. Because of this trend, desert states in the southwestern United States are experiencing an economic boom.

In contrast to traditional desert life, modern living uses up large amounts of energy and water, most of which has to be imported. Metal caravans and homes may be cheap and easy to move, but they can become unbearably hot in the glaring sun, making air-conditioning and refrigeration a necessity. The builders of homes and hotels know that residents and guests expect swimming pools and lush gardens, both of which require large amounts of water.

Greening the Desert

The earliest permanent human settlements in deserts were near other sources of water, such as springs or rivers. People soon learned, however, how to move water to other, drier locations. Over two thousand years ago, the ancient Persians built underground canals to carry water from mountain streams to deserts to grow crops. Similar **irrigation** systems are still used in some parts of the world.

GREENING DESERTS

Water from a well is used to irrigate this oasis in Sudan. People have been digging wells to obtain water for centuries. More than 1,000 years ago, the ancient Persians were using wells over 300 feet (100 m) deep. Desert peoples have developed many ingenious devices for lifting water out of wells. Water from deep wells had to be hauled up by bucket. Wells are still important in desert areas. In many places, methods of extraction have not changed for hundreds of years.

Below: A modern settlement sits in the desert of Israel. All over the world, more and more people are moving to desert areas, and new settlements are springing up. These new developments are usually built with conventional building materials and lack the special character of traditional desert homes.

Extracting Groundwater

Large amounts of water lie deep beneath parts of some deserts. This water, called groundwater, collects in layers of porous rock known as **aquifers.** In some places, water can be reached by sinking wells into the ground. With modern drilling equipment, people can bore wells to the deepest aquifers and extract huge amounts of water with mechanical pumps.

This advance in technology, however, has caused problems. A lot of the water in desert aquifers has been there for tens of thousands of years. It collected when the climate was wetter than it is now and, like oil, is not replaced when it is taken out. Traditional methods of extraction took only small amounts of water, leaving enough for future generations. Modern extraction takes out very large amounts and is often wasteful. Groundwater is being used up at a rapid rate. In some parts of the United States, acquifers are nearly exhausted, and the same is expected to happen soon in other areas.

Above: A luxury hotel on the Sinai Peninsula in Egypt offers guests a modern-day oasis. The hot, dry climate of desert areas attracts vacationers. Although tourist developments have created jobs in desert areas, they have also brought problems. Hotels, swimming pools, and gardens use up enormous amounts of water—the most precious commodity in deserts.

DESERT HUNTERS

Traditional hunting methods gave desert dwellers the means to kill a limited number of animals for food and even some for sport. Modern methods, however, are able to quickly wipe out an entire species. Desert hunters now use rifles, shotguns, and even machine guns. They chase their prey across the desert in four-wheel-drive vehicles that can catch the swiftest of animals on open ground.

Below: An Arab falconer holds a saker falcon. Falconry, the practice of training hawks to help hunters, has long been a traditional sport in the Middle East. With the arrival of oil wealth in the region, more people can afford to take up the sport. To meet the increased demand for falcons, people illegally capture and export the now endangered birds from countries in Europe, Africa, and the rest of Asia.

Left: Sport hunting has driven many animals, such as the scimitar-horned oryx, to the brink of extinction. Scimitar-horned oryx were once widespread in the Sahara and Sahel regions of North Africa. The animals were well adapted to desert conditions and could thrive in areas where the grazing was too poor for most domestic animals. They coexisted with desert nomads for centuries and until recently could be found in herds of several hundred animals. In the last 50 years, however, they have been slaughtered by hunters with automatic weapons. Only a few wild scimitar-horned oryx may still exist.

Desert animals can make easy prey for hunters. There is little vegetation for the animals to hide in. Under stress, they easily succumb to the extreme conditions. Even if they are not shot, antelopes chased across the desert may die of heat exhaustion.

Twentieth-century hunters have slaughtered much of the large animal population, especially in the deserts of North Africa and the Middle East. Antelopes such as the scimitar-horned oryx, the addax, the Dama gazelle, and the Arabian oryx and gazelle have been hunted to near extinction.

The Arabian Oryx

Arabian oryx are characterized by white coats, which reflect the sun, and long sweeping horns. To stay cool, the animals move slowly. Well adapted to desert conditions, the animals thrived for centuries on the Arabian Peninsula. But the very characteristics that helped them live in the desert made them easy prey. By the late 1950s, the Arabian oryx had become extinct in the wild.

In the following years, the few that survived in captivity were put through a breeding program in an attempt to save the species from total extinction. The animals were successfully reintroduced into their desert habitat in the 1980s. This project has been one of the few successful examples of its kind.

ENERGY FROM THE DESERT

People have been abusing desert plants and animals for decades. A desert resource that has only recently begun to be exploited is energy. The mining of desert minerals has had a huge effect on desert countries and on the world at large.

Oil and Natural Gas

The main source of energy from deserts is oil. Drilling for oil on a large scale started in the eastern United States in the 1860s. The industry expanded rapidly as oil prospectors spread out across the world in search of new deposits. Miners found large quantities of oil in the desert areas of the United States and Mexico.

Oil has brought enormous wealth and rapid modernization to many countries in the Middle East and in North Africa. At the beginning of the twentieth century, enormous reserves of oil and natural gas were discovered in the deserts of these regions. Since then, these deposits have been heavily exploited. The Middle East alone is responsible for 25 percent of the world's total oil production.

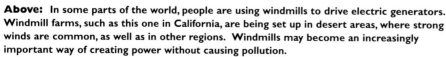
Above: In some parts of the world, people are using windmills to drive electric generators. Windmill farms, such as this one in California, are being set up in desert areas, where strong winds are common, as well as in other regions. Windmills may become an increasingly important way of creating power without causing pollution.

Fossil Fuel Pollution

Most countries are dependent on the income generated through **fossil fuels** such as oil and natural gas. But oil and natural gas are nonrenewable resources. Once they are used up, they cannot be replenished. Burning the fuels also creates pollution, especially in the form of carbon dioxide and sulfur dioxide.

Worldwide, people are looking for cleaner sources of energy. Two alternative sources of energy are **solar power** and **wind power.** Both wind and sunshine are present in large amounts in deserts. However, the technology that allows these energy sources to be harnessed has yet to be perfected.

DESERTS AS DUMPS

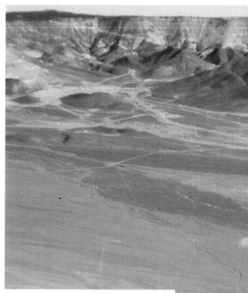

Cheap land, the absence of vegetation, and plentiful space have made deserts attractive to mining companies. Apart from fossil fuels, deserts contain a huge variety of valuable resources: iron ore, diamonds, gold, potash, phosphates, and uranium. Mining companies can make use of the large open spaces with little fear of environmental protest. For this reason, deserts have suffered from activities that would not be tolerated elsewhere.

Above: Travelers stop for the night north of Tamanrasset in the Ahaggar Mountains, in the Algerian Sahara, at the site of French overground nuclear testing in the 1950s.

Right: Sedan Crater is the result of the underground explosion of a 100 kiloton nuclear bomb in the Nevada desert on July 6, 1962. The crater is 320 feet (98 m) deep and 1,200 feet (390 m) across. The explosion displaced about 12 million tons of earth. The Nevada test site is about 65 miles (105 km) northwest of Las Vegas.

Remoteness helps to guarantee secrecy. For this reason, many of the world's major deserts have been used for nuclear weapons research. Indigenous desert people have invariably suffered from such practices.

Nuclear Legacies

The very first atomic bomb was detonated at 5:30 a.m. on July 16, 1945, in the desert near Alamogordo, New Mexico. Subsequently, the United States performed several dozen atmospheric nuclear tests at a desert site in Nevada. Each test created a heavily radioactive fallout plume that in some cases stretched across 100 miles (160 km) of desert. Hundreds more tests were carried out underground until 1992, when the Cold War nuclear rivalry between the United States and the Soviet Union came to an end.

Testing Sites

Britain undertook a series of nuclear tests at Maralinga in the Great Victoria Desert of Australia in the 1950s and 1960s. The site is still heavily contaminated with radioactivity. Many Aboriginal people, unable to read the warning signs near the test site, unknowingly hunted and fished in the area and were exposed to radioactive fallout. One report mentions the bodies of four Aborigines found in a bomb crater after one of the tests in 1963. Another article states that the British buried some radioactive debris on an Aboriginal reserve (reservation) and covered it with only a few inches of soil.

Most of the other big nuclear powers—France, the former Soviet Union, and China—have also tested their bombs in desert environments. In the 1960s, France performed 17 nuclear weapons tests in the Algerian Sahara before transferring its operations to the Pacific. India, too, exploded a nuclear bomb in the Thar Desert of Rajasthan.

Other Radioactive Threats

Nuclear weapons testing has not been the only radioactive threat to deserts. Many desert areas are rich in uranium. Uranium mining creates a host of radioactive hazards. In New Mexico the U.S. government has mined uranium from Indian reservation land to fulfill commercial and military uranium needs.

Deserts are also considered suitable sites for the dumping of nuclear waste. For years now, Carlsbad in New Mexico has been under consideration for a long-term nuclear waste disposal facility.

TOURISM IN DESERTS

More and more people are traveling the world. At the same time, people are becoming aware of unspoiled areas and interested in visiting them. All these factors mean that tourism is spreading to wilderness areas, including deserts. While some tourists come for the sun and warmth, others want to see the magnificent landforms and the variety of unique plants and animals.

Uluru, Australia

One of the most visited desert places is Uluru, or Ayers Rock, in Australia's Northern Territory. Despite being one of the most isolated places in the country, more than a quarter of a million people visit the rock each year.

This influx of visitors has brought important economic benefits to the region. Tourists spend money on hotels, restaurants, clothing, and gifts. But housing, feeding, and clearing the garbage of thousands of people at a time stresses the desert's fragile environment.

U.S. Deserts

For many years, large numbers of tourists have been visiting famous desert sites in the western United States. These include the Painted Desert and the Petrified Forest in Arizona and Bryce Canyon National Park in Utah. At these places, tourism is carefully controlled. Some areas that can be easily damaged are only accessible on foot or horseback, and the number of visitors at any one time is limited. The goal is to preserve these fragile landscapes for future generations.

Above: Uluru is one of the most important sacred sites for Australia's Aborigines. The largest single piece of stone on earth, the rock measures 5.5 miles (9 km) in circumference. Uluru, which is located near the center of Australia, is a major tourist attraction. It draws more than 250,000 visitors each year.

Right: The rising sun is reflected from Mount Olga, a huge group of uniquely-shaped rocks not far from Uluru. In 1950 Austrailia designated the Ayers Rock-Mount Olga area as Uluru National Park.

Below: Visitors tour Bryce Canyon National Park, Utah, on horseback.

The Future of Deserts

Deserts, like other environments, are changing fast because of the actions of people. Deserts face two main threats that seem to contradict each other. One problem is the destruction of natural deserts. The other is **desertification,** or the turning of nondesert areas into desert.

Desertification

Scientists disagree over how big a threat desertification represents. For many years, some experts have been particularly worried about the Sahel, a region to the south of the Sahara. They argue that too many cattle have been allowed to graze the Sahel, especially during dry years. Overgrazing, which kills off vegetation, may be turning the Sahel into desert.

But other experts are not so sure. The problem might be the result of a prolonged drought, and the land could return to normal once the weather has stabilized. In fact, both explanations may be correct. Land degradation in naturally arid areas, through overgrazing or the removal of tree cover, can make the environment more hostile than it already is.

Salinization, too, can leave formerly irrigated areas parched and lifeless. As irrigation water evaporates, it leaves behind salts that were dissolved in the water. These salts can leave a crust and render the soil useless for agriculture.

Above: Because sand shifts in the wind, desert boundaries have always moved. However, in recent years many people have feared that deserts are spreading farther and faster than before. These dunes in West Africa are smothering the trees in their paths.

Right: Soil erosion in deserts and semidesert areas is a major problem. Soils in arid areas are usually poor in quality but are able to support a sparse covering of vegetation. When this vegetation is destroyed by overgrazing or because motor vehicles drive over it too often, the soil it holds in place will be blown away in a desert storm. Without the soil, the vegetation is unable to grow back.

DESERTS ON THE MOVE

Deserts can grow, or shrink, for several different reasons. The climate may change, or people and their animals may destroy the vegetation in the dry areas bordering deserts. When the vegetation goes, the soil gets washed, or blown, away. Nothing will grow, turning what was once a green area into a desert.

Plants as Anchors

Deserts, particularly sandy ones, often move just because of the wind. Sand dunes, blown along by the wind, can travel quite quickly, burying houses, trees, and crops. For many years, people have looked for ways to stop deserts from spreading. One of the most important conservation methods is to replant vegetation with tough, quick-growing plants that do not need much water. As they grow, their roots bind the soil together and stop it from moving.

Sometimes, slow-growing plants that spread across the ground are used. These types of flora provide some shade for the seedlings of bigger plants such as trees, whose roots reach deep into the ground and provide a firm anchor. Planting is usually done by hand. In some

Above: Workers build a stone line in Burkina Faso in West Africa to hold shifting sand and soil in place. Even though they are sometimes low, stone lines can also stop rainwater from running off. In deserts, rainfall is often sudden and very fierce. Much of the water runs off into dry stream and river beds before it can soak into the ground. Stone lines like these can hold up the water long enough for it to soak in and water plants.

parts of the world, grass seed has been sown from aircraft. This method is quicker but is also much more expensive.

If the ground is eroding quickly or if sand dunes are moving too fast, stone walls or wooden fences can be used as barriers. These structures can hold up the moving soil long enough to allow plants to get a firm grip. These systems are also used on sandy beaches and sand dunes in nondesert environments.

Left: A desert dweller plants trees in Mauritania, Africa. As well as stopping erosion, trees in deserts provide valuable firewood, food for livestock, and windbreaks for tents and houses. However, trees need careful attention after they have been planted. Often trees used in schemes to stop desertification die from neglect.

DESERT PARKS

One way to preserve deserts is to turn sections of them into national parks or reserves—places where environmentally hazardous activities such as sport hunting and mining are prohibited. Many desert parks and reserves, some of which cover thousands of square miles, now exist throughout the world. The areas serve to protect unique landscapes, to preserve rare and endangered plants and animals, and to permit indigenous peoples to maintain a traditional way of life. In many cases, the needs of indigenous peoples who live in the parks or reserves must concur with the needs of the area's wild animals and plants.

Operating Costs

Wealthy countries such as Australia and the United States spend a lot of money making sure their parks are properly run. The money is needed to pay attendants and to provide facilities for people who visit the parks. However, many important desert parks are in countries that cannot afford all the expenses of running a reserve.

The Aïr and the Ténéré Nature Reserve

One major desert park is the Aïr and Ténéré Nature Reserve in Niger, in the central part of the Sahara. This enormous reserve covers nearly 20 million acres (8 million hectares) and protects the last wild populations of two of the largest of deserts animals—the scimitar-horned oryx and the addax.

Above: Monument Valley Navajo Tribal Park lies within the Navajo Indian Reservation in Utah and Arizona. Although many interesting plants and animals live there, Monument Valley is best known for its wonderful landscape of eroded rocks. These shapes are familiar to movie-goers all over the world through the many Westerns that have been filmed in the valley.

Although the scimitar-horned oryx and the addax live in zoos, the Aïr and Ténéré reserve is the last hope for these animals to survive in the wild. Other rare animals living in the reserve include Dama gazelles, aoudads (Barbary sheep), and cheetahs. Few people visit the reserve because it is so inaccessible. But the government of Niger is counting on a gradual increase in the number of tourists, whose visitation fees will help pay for the park's operating costs.

Deserts Are Special

Some people who have never been to deserts find it hard to understand their special qualities. But those who have find it hard to forget them. The fighting spirit of desert peoples is balanced by their hospitality to strangers. Urbanites often find that visiting a desert is a moving, spiritual experience.

On a crowded planet, deserts are among the last of the true wilderness areas. A desert is a unique and harsh environment, where living things have developed resourceful survival techniques to cope with extreme conditions. The desert environment gives shape and meaning to the lives of its people, who understand better than most how to live off of it without destroying it.

Above: A herd of addaxes rest in the Aïr and Ténéré reserve in Niger. Like the scimitar-horned oryx, the addax was a common antelope in the Sahara until overhunting recently brought it to near extinction. The animal was even better adapted than the oryx to life in the very hottest and driest parts of the desert. The last wild population of addaxes lives off-limits to hunters in the Aïr and Ténéré reserve.

A SMALL DESERT RESERVE

Not all desert parks and reserves are large. Some small areas can be very important for preserving rare plants and animals. One small but important reserve is the Berenty Reserve in the spiny desert in southern Madagascar. The area covers only 600 acres (250 hectares) but attracts tourists and scientists from all over the world. They come to see the Verreaux's sifakas and the ring-tailed lemurs. Three other sorts of lemur also live in the reserve, as well as a breeding colony of radiated tortoises. Bird-watchers can examine more than 70 types of birds found only on or near the island.

Glossary

aquifers: Layers of porous rock beneath the ground in which water collects.

desertification: The process of becoming a desert. Desertification can be caused by prolonged drought or the removal of vegetation.

drought: A prolonged absence of rain.

ephemeral: A plant that grows, flowers, and dies in a few days.

erg: A desert region of shifting sand.

erosion: The wearing away of land surfaces by the action of wind and water.

fossil fuel: A fuel, such as coal or oil, that has been formed from prehistoric plant and animal remains.

gers: Circular, domed tents made of skins and cloth stretched over a wooden frame. Gers are used by nomads in the Gobi.

groundwater: Water that collects in layers of porous rock beneath the desert and that can be extracted by digging or drilling.

irrigation: The practice of transporting water by artificial means, such as canals, from lakes or rivers to crops.

nomads: People who travel from place to place within a defined territory to make the best use of scarce or seasonal foods and other resources.

oasis: A fertile place in a desert watered either by natural sources such as rivers or springs or by wells or irrigation canals.

precipitation: Water that falls to the ground in the form of rain, snow, or hail.

reservations: Areas of land set aside by the U.S. government for Native Americans.

salinization: The saturation of land by salt deposits often left behind after irrigation water evaporates.

sand dunes: Hills of sand formed by the action of wind.

savanna: Tropical grassland with scattered trees and bushes.

Silk Road: An ancient trading route between Europe and China that passed through the Gobi.

solar power: Energy generated from the sun.

succulents: Desert plants, including the cactus family, that can store water in order to survive long periods of drought.

tubers: The swollen undergrown stems of some plants, such as potatoes.

wind power: A source of energy generated by harnessing the power of the wind.

Index